Echos of Orwell

John Shenton

Published by John Shenton, 2024.

While every precaution has been taken in the preparation of this book, the publisher assumes no responsibility for errors or omissions, or for damages resulting from the use of the information contained herein.

ECHOS OF ORWELL

First edition. September 28, 2024.

Copyright © 2024 John Shenton.

ISBN: 979-8224065974

Written by John Shenton.

Also by John Shenton

Business Plan Basics
The Bahamas - More Islands and Recipes Than You Expect!
Collected Musings from Bricks and Mortar to E-commerce
The Smart City Odyssey: Unveiling the Secrets to Traveller-Centric
Software
The Dragon's Gambit: China's Bid for Global Dominance and the
Western Response
Silent Weapon
Business Basics: Money Sources
Influx
Fried Chips
Mandates, Motors, and Misinformation
Echos of Orwell
Control and Chaos
The Empire's Warning: What Rome's Fall Tells Us About the West
Today

Table of Contents

Foreword

I was born in post-war Britain, a time when the aftermath of a global conflict shaped our collective understanding of democracy, freedom, and, most importantly, free speech. Having grown up in this era, I have always believed that the ability to speak openly, to challenge the prevailing norms, and to express dissent were rights that formed the bedrock of a free society. It was a freedom that many of us took for granted, believing it was inherent to our way of life. Yet, as I look at the world today, I see alarming signs that this vital liberty is being slowly but surely eroded, not just in the UK, but across the Western world.

"Echoes of Orwell: The Erosion of Free Speech and the Silencing of Dissent" is my attempt to chart this troubling trend. Each chapter of this book paints a picture of how the forces of censorship and control once the hallmarks of authoritarian regimes are creeping into the liberal democracies, we hold dear. From the United States to Europe, Australia, and even my own United Kingdom, I see daily examples of governments and institutions tightening the reins on what can be said and who can say it. I have witnessed the rise of a culture where fear of offending others, or of being branded a dissenter, now overrides the freedom to speak one's mind.

George Orwell warned us of this long ago. His seminal works, *1984* and *Animal Farm* are more relevant today than ever before. In *1984*, Orwell depicted a society where truth was manipulated, dissent was punished, and the mere act of thinking critically was enough to label one as a traitor. It is a chilling vision, but one that echoes through our current reality. The parallels are clear, and throughout the chapters of this book, I have endeavoured to show how these warnings are manifesting in the present day.

In **Chapter 11: What Can Be Done?** I call upon voters and citizens to act before it is too late. The rights we cherish are not inevitable they must be defended. I offer practical steps to resist the encroachment of censorship: voting for politicians who prioritise free speech, supporting independent media, and standing firm against the culture of fear that seeks to silence dissent. Orwell's message was clear passive acceptance is dangerous, and it is up to us to challenge the trends that threaten our freedoms.

In **Chapter 10: Convergence with China**, I explore the disturbing convergence between Western democracies and China's authoritarian speech control. Having spent decades observing the Chinese model, it is shocking to see how Western governments have begun to justify censorship in the name of "national security," "social harmony," and "public order." The systematic control of speech is no longer the preserve of overtly authoritarian regimes it is becoming a reality here in the West, where even our democratic values are being warped to suppress dissent.

I am deeply concerned about the growing acceptance of speech regulation in places like Australia and Europe, as explored in **Chapters 6 and 5**. While these laws are often introduced under the guise of protecting minorities or preserving public order, the consequences of their overreach are becoming evident. Even in the UK, where free speech has been a proud tradition, we have seen public order laws used to police what can and cannot be said, as outlined in **Chapter 4**. These measures are not simply about preserving social harmony they are about control.

I believe that we cannot afford to remain silent. The erosion of free speech is not an inevitable consequence of modern society. We have seen, in places like the United States and Canada, that the balance between inclusion and free expression is a delicate one. As explored in **Chapters 2 and 3**, there is a growing trend to prioritise protection over freedom, often to the detriment of the latter. Orwell's concept of "thoughtcrime" is no longer a dystopian fantasy it is a reality we must grapple with today.

In **Chapter 9**, I examine the resistance that is forming. Some are fighting back against grassroots movements, civil libertarians, and individuals who, like me, recognise the dangers of allowing free speech to be curtailed. The fight is not over, but it requires each of us to stand firm against the tide of censorship.

This book is not just a warning, but a call to action. Free speech is a cornerstone of our democracy. Without it, we lose the ability to debate, to challenge, and to grow as a society. The future of our free expression rests in our hands. By recognising the warning signs, learning from Orwell's prescient works, and taking decisive action, we can preserve the right to speak freely and secure the future of democratic debate for generations to come.

This is my plea, not just as an author, but as someone who has lived through a time when free speech was a given. Let us not lose it now.

John Shenton

Chapter 1: Introduction – A New Era of Censorship?

Free Speech: A Cornerstone of Western Democracies

For centuries, the concept of free speech has been heralded as a foundational pillar of liberty within Western democracies. The ability to express one's thoughts, opinions, and beliefs without fear of government repression is not only a human right but a hallmark of a healthy, functioning society. In ancient Athens, the birthplace of democratic ideals, the concept of "parrhesia" free and open speech was revered as essential to the civic life of its citizens. Later, philosophers like John Locke and Voltaire emphasized the importance of free expression as vital to individual liberty and societal progress. Through centuries of political evolution, many of these principles were enshrined in the legal frameworks of modern democracies.

The United States' First Amendment to the Constitution is perhaps the most iconic embodiment of this ideal, guaranteeing freedom of speech, press, and assembly. The UK's history of intellectual discourse and political debate, including figures such as John Stuart Mill, further solidified these rights within the public consciousness. Similar protections emerged across Europe, Canada, Australia, and other democratic nations, reinforcing the principle that societies flourish when individuals can freely express their thoughts even, especially when those thoughts challenge authority or provoke discomfort.

However, as the 21st century progresses, the veneration of free speech in many of these nations appears to be transforming. Recent years have seen the emergence of a new kind of censorship one that is more subtle and often cloaked in the language of safety, inclusivity, and security. While the historical understanding of censorship invoked images of authoritarian regimes and oppressive state apparatuses, today's forms are more complex, blending legislative, social, and technological measures. In many cases, governments and institutions are placing new limits on speech, purportedly to protect certain groups or to prevent harm, yet these measures raise profound questions about the balance between security and freedom. Are we witnessing a gradual erosion of the very liberties that Western societies have long championed?

A Gradual Shift: The Rise of Modern Censorship

The changes have not been abrupt or overt. Instead, they have crept into the political, legal, and social fabric of Western democracies, often couched in the language of protection or progress. Governments, particularly those with left-leaning ideologies, are increasingly imposing restrictions on speech that challenge the prevailing consensus or question the status quo.

In the United States, debates over so-called "hate speech" legislation have gained significant traction. While the First Amendment still provides robust protections for free expression, there has been a growing movement to carve out exceptions for speech deemed harmful to specific groups based on race, gender, sexual orientation, or religion. The rise of social media platforms, where vast amounts of public discourse now take place, has also led to calls for greater regulation of online speech, often in the name of combating misinformation or curbing extremist ideologies.

In Canada, laws such as Bill C-16, which added gender identity and expression to the list of prohibited grounds for discrimination, have sparked heated debates over the boundaries of free speech. Critics have raised concerns that such laws may compel individuals to use certain forms of speech or risk punishment, while proponents argue that these measures are necessary to protect marginalized communities.

The United Kingdom has also seen an uptick in laws aimed at regulating online and public discourse. The UK's Public Order Act of 1986, originally designed to address violent riots, has been increasingly used to police "offensive" speech. Recent expansions of the law have empowered authorities to arrest individuals for social media posts that are considered "grossly offensive" or likely to cause harm. Many argue that such measures, while well-intentioned, risk stifling legitimate expression, creating a chilling effect on public discourse.

Across Europe, the European Union's Digital Services Act aims to regulate large online platforms, requiring them to remove illegal content and misinformation more swiftly. This initiative reflects a broader trend within European governments to combat what they view as harmful speech online. However, critics warn that these regulations could enable greater state control over what is permissible speech, leaving the door open for misuse and overreach.

Australia, too, has joined this global shift, enacting laws such as the Online Safety Act, which grants the government greater authority to order the removal of online content deemed harmful. While intended to protect children and vulnerable individuals from exploitation or bullying, such laws raise questions about who decides what constitutes "harmful" content and whether these mechanisms could be used to suppress dissent.

Legislative and Social Measures: A Balancing Act?

One of the central tensions in these debates revolves around the question of balance. How can governments protect vulnerable communities and promote civil discourse without infringing on the fundamental right to free speech? Where is the line between legitimate regulation of harmful content and authoritarian suppression of dissenting voices?

The rise of "cancel culture" has further complicated the landscape. What began as a means of holding individuals and institutions accountable for harmful behaviour has, in some cases, morphed into a powerful tool for silencing dissent. Prominent figures in academia, journalism, and politics have found themselves marginalized or professionally ruined for expressing unpopular opinions. While many see this as an organic, socially driven form of accountability, others argue that it represents a troubling new form of censorship, one driven not by governments but by social and corporate pressures.

This dynamic is perhaps most evident in the debates over "misinformation." In an era of mass digital communication, the spread of false information is undeniably a significant problem. Governments and tech companies alike have grappled with how to curtail the spread of conspiracy theories, pseudoscience, and other harmful narratives. However, attempts to regulate misinformation raise difficult questions: Who decides what counts as misinformation? Could this power be misused to suppress legitimate dissent or inconvenient truths?

Orwell's Vision: Are We Living in "1984"?

These recent trends have led many to draw comparisons to George Orwell's classic dystopian novels *1984* and *Animal Farm*. In *1984*, Orwell described a society in which the state, through its omnipresent surveillance and control of information, crushed all dissent. The concept of "thoughtcrime" looms large in the novel citizens are not only punished for their actions but for their very thoughts, should they deviate from the Party's approved doctrine. Central to Orwell's vision is the idea that language itself can be manipulated to suppress dissent, a concept he famously explored through the invention of "Newspeak" a language designed to eliminate the possibility of rebellious thoughts.

Animal Farm, though different in tone and setting, similarly explores the idea that once ideals of equality and fairness are corrupted by those in power, they can become tools of oppression. The phrase "All animals are equal, but some animals are more equal than others" resonates today, as debates over free speech, power, and censorship echo across modern democracies.

In both novels, Orwell warned of the dangers of concentrated power and the silencing of dissent warnings that seem eerily prescient in today's political climate. The manipulation of language, the policing of thought, and the use of fear to control populations are themes that resonate in discussions about the limits of free speech today. Are we inching closer to an Orwellian reality, where speech is tightly controlled, not through overt repression, but through a combination of legislative constraints, social pressures, and technological control?

Setting the Stage: Themes of This Book

The purpose of this book is to explore these pressing questions in greater depth. As we move through its chapters, we will delve into the specific legislative measures, social dynamics, and historical precedents that have shaped the current moment. We will examine how censorship in its many forms whether state-imposed or socially driven threatens the very foundation of Western democratic values.

The echo of Orwell's dystopian vision serves as both a cautionary tale and a lens through which we can view our current reality. The line between protection and oppression is often razor-thin, and as this book will argue, the defence of free speech no matter how difficult or uncomfortable it may be is essential for the preservation of liberty. If we continue down this path of ever-tightening control, we may find ourselves living in a world that resembles Orwell's worst fears: a society where dissent is gagged, and the freedom to speak one's mind is but a distant memory.

Conclusion

As we embark on this exploration, the question remains: Are we truly entering a new era of censorship, where the ideals of free speech once held so dear by Western democracies are at risk of becoming relics of the past? This book will not only seek to answer that question but also to illuminate the broader consequences of this shift. If the trend continues, it may not be long before Orwell's warnings become our reality. A fitting George Orwell quote that encapsulates the themes of the chapter comes from his essay *"The Freedom of the Press"*, which was initially intended as a preface to *Animal Farm*:

> *"If liberty means anything at all it means the right to tell people what they do not want to hear."*

This quote reflects the essence of free speech—the idea that true liberty involves the defence of unpopular or uncomfortable opinions, even when they challenge prevailing norms. It underscores the central argument of the chapter, where the balance between protection and the freedom to dissent is at the heart of the new forms of censorship taking shape in modern democracies.

The challenge, then, is clear: Can we protect the rights of individuals to speak freely while ensuring that speech itself does not become a tool of harm or oppression? Or will the pendulum swing too far, silencing voices in the name of protection?

Chapter 2: The United States – The First Amendment Under Siege

The First Amendment to the United States Constitution is perhaps the most celebrated clause in the nation's founding document, guaranteeing the essential freedoms that form the bedrock of American democracy. It proclaims: "Congress shall make no law... abridging the freedom of speech, or of the press." For over two centuries, this right has been fiercely guarded, often held up as an example to the world of America's commitment to liberty. However, in recent years, this hallowed principle has come under increasing scrutiny and strain. This chapter delves into the challenges confronting the First Amendment today, focusing on political correctness, cancel culture, government intervention in media, and the role of social media giants in shaping and, some argue, restricting public discourse.

The Role of the First Amendment in American Identity

Historically, free speech in the United States has been considered not just a legal guarantee but an ethical and cultural ideal. It is woven into the fabric of American identity and perceived as a universal right that upholds the marketplace of ideas. The country's courts have repeatedly defended this ideal, from cases involving political speech to offensive expressions. The understanding has always been that the best antidote to bad speech is more speech, rather than censorship. The tension that exists today, however, is whether this marketplace has been compromised and whether certain voices are being silenced through more insidious and decentralized means than government censorship.

Political Correctness and the Boundaries of Acceptable Speech

A crucial factor contributing to the perceived erosion of free speech is the rise of political correctness. Originally intended to foster an environment of respect and inclusivity, political correctness in its more extreme form has been criticized for stifling dissent. The parameters of "acceptable" discourse have, over time, narrowed as certain viewpoints, particularly on contentious social issues such as race, gender, and sexuality, are increasingly labelled as offensive or harmful.

George Orwell's concept of *newspeak* in *1984*, introduced in Chapter 1 of this book, serves as a pertinent analogy here. In Orwell's dystopia, language is manipulated to constrict the range of thought. Words are eliminated or their meanings altered to ensure ideological conformity. While the United States is not eliminating words from its lexicon, a similar mechanism of social pressure has emerged, where expressing politically incorrect opinions can lead to professional and personal repercussions. This dynamic of self-censorship, driven by the fear of social ostracism, has created an atmosphere in which people are less willing to engage in open, honest dialogue. As a result, what was once the expansive liberty of free speech has been circumscribed by unspoken rules dictating what can and cannot be said.

Cancel Culture: A New Form of Social Censorship

At the heart of this shift is the phenomenon known as *cancel culture*. While political correctness might create a nebulous boundary around acceptable speech, cancel culture enforces it with swift and sometimes ruthless consequences. Public figures be they celebrities, politicians, or everyday citizens have been "cancelled" for statements or actions deemed problematic, often with little room for redemption or dialogue. The immediacy of social media amplifies this trend, where viral outrage can lead to the erasure of reputations, careers, and even lives in mere hours.

Cancel culture, some argue, reflects Orwellian tendencies in modern society, where public discourse is policed not by a totalitarian government but by an amorphous collective wielding the power of social media. It creates a chilling effect: individuals become reluctant to express opinions that might fall outside the accepted mainstream for fear of cancellation. As a result, entire avenues of debate and discourse are closed off, limiting the public's ability to engage with diverse viewpoints.

In this sense, cancel culture can be seen as an outgrowth of the Orwellian principle of *thoughtcrime*. While the government may not be directly involved, the principles of social conformity, shaming, and punishment for unorthodox ideas bear a striking resemblance to Orwell's vision of a society where deviation from the accepted narrative is met with severe consequences.

Social Media Giants: The New Gatekeepers of Public Discourse

If political correctness and cancel culture have narrowed the scope of individual expression, social media platforms have, in many ways, become the arbiters of public discourse. Facebook, Twitter, YouTube, and others have unprecedented control over what billions of people read, watch, and discuss. As privately owned companies, these platforms are not bound by the First Amendment's protections, which apply to government action, not corporate policy. Yet their decisions about what content to allow or ban can have enormous consequences for free speech.

Legislative actions aimed at addressing misinformation, hate speech, and other harmful content have led to more aggressive moderation practices. While these efforts may be well-intentioned, they also raise important questions about the balance between protecting users from harm and ensuring a free flow of ideas. Platforms often employ "fact-checkers" and algorithms to flag and remove content, but these systems are far from perfect. Algorithms can be biased, reflecting the ideological leanings of their creators, and "fact-checkers" are human and therefore fallible.

One example is the debate over free speech in the context of parental rights that has taken on a new dimension under the Biden - Harris administration, particularly concerning how parents engage with school boards and local educational authorities. The issue has gained national attention, with many parents voicing concerns over curricula, school policies, and the influence of various ideological perspectives on their children's education. Some argue that the Biden administration's response, characterized by increased scrutiny of parent activism, infringes on the fundamental right of free speech and amounts to a form of government overreach.

Central to the controversy are the Department of Justice (DOJ) and the Department of Education's actions in response to heightened confrontations at school board meetings across the country. A key moment came when the National School Boards Association (NSBA) sent a letter to the administration, likening the actions of some parents to domestic terrorism, prompting a DOJ investigation into potential threats against school officials. This move, critics argue, is part of a broader pattern of intimidation aimed at silencing dissent and stifling free expression, especially among parents concerned about what they see as ideological indoctrination in public schools.

Proponents of the administration's actions claim they are necessary to maintain order and protect school officials from harassment and threats, but many parents and civil liberties advocates view the response as an overreach, chilling legitimate forms of protest and debate. They argue that in a democratic society, parents have the right to participate in their children's education, express their concerns, and challenge policies they disagree with without fear of government surveillance or retaliation. This issue highlights the tension between free speech, safety, and government authority in modern America, with parental rights becoming a flashpoint in broader cultural and political battles over education.

These dynamics recall *1984*'s Ministry of Truth, which was tasked with editing and revising information to reflect the government's preferred narrative. Today's fact-checkers, while ostensibly serving the public interest, wield similar power over the flow of information. Decisions about what is "true" or "false" can be subjective and influenced by political or social biases. The use of algorithms to filter content similarly recalls Orwell's warnings about the dangers of centralized control over information.

Government Intervention and the Media Landscape

While the United States government is constitutionally barred from restricting speech directly, its influence over media and public discourse has not disappeared. In recent years, politicians and lawmakers on both sides of the political aisle have exerted pressure on media companies and tech platforms to control what is deemed harmful speech. The debate over Section 230 of the Communications Decency Act, which provides liability protection to tech companies for content posted by their users, has led to calls for reform that would compel social media platforms to exercise more control over content moderation. However, critics argue that this may pave the way for government overreach, effectively leading to censorship by proxy.

Government actions aimed at combating disinformation whether through proposed legislation or alliances with tech companies have blurred the line between public and private control of speech. In some cases, this has resulted in platforms becoming quasi-governmental entities tasked with enforcing evolving norms around speech. While the intentions may be to safeguard democracy from foreign interference, hate speech, or misinformation, there are growing concerns that such interventions could create a slippery slope toward authoritarian-style control over information.

Orwell's Legacy in Modern America

George Orwell's warning in *1984* about the manipulation of language and thought to control society is uncannily relevant to modern America. The rise of political correctness, cancel culture, the consolidation of social media power, and increasing government intervention in media all reflect elements of Orwell's nightmare vision. In this environment, the foundational principle of free speech, long considered inviolable, is increasingly under siege.

As we saw in Chapter 1, the erosion of free speech is not limited to the United States; it is a phenomenon seen across Western democracies. However, in the United States, where the First Amendment is so deeply embedded in the national psyche, the tension between free speech and its limitations is particularly stark. As this chapter has explored, the threats to free expression today are complex, decentralized, and sometimes difficult to discern. They do not come from an overtly authoritarian government but from a convergence of social, technological, and political forces that together have made the free marketplace of ideas far less open than it once was.

In the chapters to follow, this book will continue to explore how these forces are reshaping the notion of free speech, not only in America but across the globe. The questions raised here about political correctness, cancel culture, the role of social media giants, and government intervention will remain central to understanding how free societies grapple with the ever-evolving challenge of protecting the right to speak freely in a world where the boundaries of expression are constantly shifting.

Chapter 3: Canada – The Rise of Speech Regulation in the Name of Inclusion

A Tradition of Free Speech

Canada, a nation often celebrated for its multiculturalism and emphasis on human rights, has historically placed great value on free expression. Rooted in its Charter of Rights and Freedoms, Section 2(b) guarantees "freedom of thought, belief, opinion and expression, including freedom of the press and other media of communication." Much like its southern neighbour, the United States, Canada has long regarded free speech as a cornerstone of democracy. However, in recent decades, this tradition has been increasingly tempered by legislative efforts aimed at promoting social inclusion, with a particular focus on protecting marginalized groups.

While the Charter provides a robust defence of free speech, it also contains significant qualifications. The Canadian government has enacted hate speech laws, human rights codes, and, more recently, legislation concerning gender identity and expression, such as the controversial Bill C-16. These legal measures, designed to protect vulnerable groups from discrimination and violence, have simultaneously sparked heated debate over the balance between safeguarding inclusion and upholding broader speech rights. Critics argue that Canada's pursuit of social justice has, at times, veered into the territory of censorship, stifling legitimate debate and dissent in the process.

Drawing on the themes of equality and power explored in George Orwell's *Animal Farm*, this chapter will examine how well-meaning policies, intended to create a more inclusive society, have evolved into tools for controlling discourse. It will argue that, like Orwell's pigs in *Animal Farm*, who gradually subvert the very principles of equality they originally championed, Canadian policymakers risk transforming initiatives aimed at fostering inclusion into mechanisms of speech regulation that disproportionately empower the state.

Hate Speech Laws: An Erosion of Free Expression?

Canada's approach to regulating hate speech is one of the most prominent examples of its attempts to balance free speech and inclusion. Section 319 of the Criminal Code of Canada criminalizes the "willful promotion of hatred" against identifiable groups based on characteristics such as race, religion, and sexual orientation. Proponents of these laws argue that they are necessary to protect marginalized communities from harm, preventing the spread of dangerous ideologies that could lead to violence. Yet, critics contend that such laws risk infringing on free speech, suppressing legitimate discussion and debate on sensitive topics.

Unlike the United States, where the First Amendment provides near-absolute protection for free speech including hate speech Canada takes a more interventionist approach. Supporters of Canada's hate speech laws often frame them as necessary tools for building an inclusive society. However, critics maintain that the laws cast a chilling effect on public discourse, as the broad language used in the legislation leaves room for subjective interpretation. This has led to accusations that these laws are being weaponized to silence opposing viewpoints under the guise of promoting tolerance.

In Chapter 2, we examined how the United States' First Amendment is under siege, with digital platforms and social media companies increasingly curbing speech in ways that echo the themes of Orwell's *1984*. In contrast, Canada's state-sponsored interventions into free speech, particularly through hate speech legislation, reflect a different but equally Orwellian dynamic. In *Animal Farm*, the pigs initially claim that all animals are equal, but they gradually reserve special privileges for themselves, using their newfound power to suppress dissent. Similarly, while Canada's hate speech laws may have been introduced with the best of intentions, they have also allowed the government to assume an ever-expanding role in policing speech, ostensibly in the name of protecting equality.

Bill C-16: Gender Identity and Expression Law

Perhaps no piece of legislation in recent Canadian history has generated as much controversy over free speech as Bill C-16. Passed in 2017, the bill added "gender identity or expression" as a prohibited ground of discrimination under the Canadian Human Rights Act and the Criminal Code. The bill was initially intended to protect transgender individuals from discrimination and hate crimes. However, its critics argued that it could also compel speech by requiring individuals to use specific gender pronouns, thereby infringing on their freedom of expression.

The debate over Bill C-16 gained international attention, largely due to the outspoken opposition of figures like University of Toronto professor Jordan Peterson. Peterson argued that the law represented a dangerous precedent, one in which the government could mandate what individuals must say, rather than merely prohibiting harmful speech. He warned that the legislation was a form of "compelled speech," echoing the authoritarian controls Orwell warned about in *1984*. While supporters of the bill emphasized the need for inclusivity and respect for gender diversity, its opponents saw it as part of a broader trend toward regulating language and suppressing dissent.

The parallels to *Animal Farm* are evident here, too. In Orwell's novella, the animals' original commitment to equality is slowly eroded as the pigs introduce rules that benefit themselves while punishing those who do not conform. The commandments, which once promised fairness for all, are altered to suit the pigs' growing power. In the same way, Bill C-16, while ostensibly designed to promote inclusion and fairness, has raised concerns that it grants the government excessive authority to dictate the boundaries of acceptable speech. This has led many to argue that the legislation reflects a shift from the protection of individual rights to the imposition of ideological conformity.

Other Legislative Acts: The Broader Trend of Speech Regulation

Bill C-16 is not the only example of how Canada has sought to regulate speech in the name of inclusion. The Canadian Human Rights Commission and various provincial human rights tribunals have played an increasingly active role in adjudicating cases related to speech, particularly in the areas of online harassment and hate speech. The rise of social media has intensified these efforts, as governments have introduced new policies aimed at curbing online hate speech and misinformation. Critics argue that these measures amount to an ever-growing encroachment on free speech, with the government taking on the role of arbiter of what constitutes acceptable discourse.

Synopsis of Bill C-63 (Online Harms Act):

Bill C-63, introduced in February 2024, is an initiative by Canada's left-leaning government to regulate harmful content on online platforms. The legislation seeks to hold social media, adult content, and live-streaming services accountable for managing content deemed harmful, specifically in seven areas: non-consensual intimate material, child exploitation, incitement of violence, hatred, terrorism, and content that bullies or endangers children.

The Act proposes the creation of a **Digital Safety Commission of Canada**, a five-member body tasked with enforcing regulations, investigating complaints, and issuing penalties. Violations can result in fines of up to 8% of a company's global revenue or $25 million. Online platforms are also required to proactively remove harmful content and maintain records to prove compliance with the law.

In addition to creating new duties for online platforms, Bill C-63 amends several existing laws, including the Criminal Code and the Canadian Human Rights Act, to strengthen penalties for hate crimes, extend reporting obligations for internet providers, and increase the statute of limitations for prosecuting child pornography offences.

While the Bill is positioned as a safeguard against online harms, it has yet to pass through the full legislative process and remains subject to debate in the House of Commons and the Senate.

Commentary on Free Speech and Political Bias:

Bill C-63 raises substantial concerns about its potential to infringe on free speech, particularly given the broad powers it grants to regulatory bodies and its reliance on subjective definitions of "harmful content." Categories such as "content that foments hatred" or "content that incites violence" are open to interpretation and could easily be exploited by those in power to silence dissent or unpopular views.

The fact that the legislation comes from a left-leaning government, combined with the growing influence of politically aligned activists, adds to the unease. Critics argue that this could lead to selective enforcement of the Act, with those in power determining what qualifies as harmful speech while overlooking or excusing content that aligns with their political views. The ability to shut down or censor content under the guise of preventing harm echoes the warnings of George Orwell, who foresaw the dangers of authoritarian overreach masquerading as protection for the public good.

Orwell's concerns about the state controlling information to suppress dissent seem relevant here. By giving the government, via the Digital Safety Commission, authority to determine what constitutes "hatred" or "extremism," the Bill risks becoming a tool for political censorship. Even with the establishment of a Digital Safety Ombudsperson, the transparency and fairness of these decisions remain questionable. If political bias seeps into how harmful speech is defined or enforced, any appearance of fairness will be negated, as critics fear that only certain viewpoints opposing the political establishment may be silenced.

The risk is that platforms, fearing the steep penalties for non-compliance, will over-moderate content and pre-emptively suppress free expression. In a politically charged environment, this could disproportionately affect individuals and groups whose opinions run counter to the dominant ideology. As a result, the Act could create a chilling effect where self-censorship becomes the norm, and public discourse is stifled, all in the name of protecting against "harm."

In conclusion, while the Online Harms Act is designed to protect against real online dangers, its vague definitions, combined with the political leanings of those enforcing it, raise legitimate concerns about its potential for misuse. The balance between protecting individuals from genuine threats and ensuring free speech is not quashed by ideological bias remains precarious.

In Chapter 1, I discussed how Western democracies are increasingly grappling with the tension between free speech and the desire to protect vulnerable populations. Canada's experience provides a case study of how this tension plays out in practice. Orwell's warnings about the dangers of authoritarianism are particularly relevant here. In *Animal Farm*, the pigs' initial commitment to equality is gradually replaced by a more insidious form of control, one in which dissent is stifled, and the promise of fairness is manipulated to serve the interests of those in power. Similarly, Canada's efforts to promote inclusion through speech regulation have, in some instances, morphed into mechanisms for restricting freedom of expression, with the government assuming greater authority to dictate what can and cannot be said.

Conclusion: A Cautionary Tale

Canada's approach to speech regulation in the name of inclusion offers a cautionary tale about the potential dangers of well-meaning policies. While the desire to protect marginalized groups from harm is both noble and necessary, it must be balanced against the need to preserve free expression as a fundamental right. As Orwell's *Animal Farm* illustrates, the pursuit of equality can sometimes lead to the erosion of individual freedoms, with those in power using the rhetoric of inclusion to justify ever-greater control over public discourse.

Canada's experience serves as a warning that, even in societies that pride themselves on their commitment to human rights, the line between protection and censorship can be perilously thin. As this book has explored, from the United States' battle over the First Amendment to the broader trend of censorship in Western democracies, the erosion of free speech often begins with the best of intentions. Yet, as Orwell understood all too well, the path to authoritarianism is often paved with such intentions. In the case of Canada, the rise of speech regulation in the name of inclusion reflects the ongoing struggle to balance equality with the preservation of individual freedoms, a struggle that will continue to shape the future of free expression in the years to come.

Chapter 4: The United Kingdom – The Chilling Effects of Public Order Laws

The United Kingdom, a nation long celebrated for its robust traditions of free speech, now finds itself grappling with a paradox. On the one hand, the UK's legal framework still champions individual liberty, while on the other, it increasingly curtails the very expressions it once protected. This erosion of free speech has unfolded gradually, under the guise of maintaining public order and protecting vulnerable groups. As I explored in earlier chapters, such as in Canada's case (Chapter 3), this trajectory is by no means unique to Britain. Yet, the UK's particular history and legal landscape offer a unique case study of how public order laws, hate speech provisions, and the policing of so-called "hate incidents" have transformed the environment for public discourse.

The Evolution of Public Order Laws: A Legal Quagmire

To understand the chilling effects of public order laws in the UK, one must first look at the statutes that undergird them. Historically, the UK has had various laws designed to keep public peace, but over the past few decades, these have increasingly been used to control speech rather than action. One of the most significant laws in this regard is the Public Order Act 1986, which originally sought to curb violence and disorder but has since become a tool for prosecuting "offensive" speech.

Section 5 of the Act has been a focal point of criticism. It makes it an offence to use "threatening, abusive or insulting words or behaviour" that could cause "harassment, alarm, or distress." This language, which seems reasonable at first glance, has been weaponized to silence speech that is simply provocative, controversial, or offensive to some. For instance, people have been arrested for holding up signs that others found offensive, or for expressing contentious opinions in public forums. The threshold for what constitutes "abusive" or "insulting" is vague and subject to interpretation, making it a potent tool for those seeking to suppress dissenting voices.

In this context, the parallels to Orwell's *1984* are striking. Orwell's concept of *thoughtcrime* the notion that even thinking the wrong thoughts could be a punishable offence finds a modern echo in the UK's legal framework. While the government may not (yet) prosecute individuals for their internal thoughts, the line between policing speech and policing thought is becoming increasingly blurred. The broad and ambiguous definitions enshrined in these laws enable the state to clamp down on speech that challenges the prevailing orthodoxy, whether it be political, religious, or cultural.

Hate Speech Laws and the "Hate Incident" Phenomenon

A crucial extension of these public order laws is the introduction and enforcement of hate speech provisions. In the UK, hate speech is defined as any speech that incites hatred against a person based on characteristics such as race, religion, sexual orientation, or gender identity. On the surface, the intent behind hate speech laws is noble: to protect marginalized communities from discrimination and abuse. However, in practice, these laws often serve to suppress not just hateful rhetoric, but legitimate debate and critical discourse.

A particularly troubling development in this area is the use of "hate incidents" to police thought. Hate incidents, as defined by UK law enforcement, are events where the victim or anyone else perceives an act to be motivated by hostility or prejudice, even if no crime has been committed. The subjective nature of this definition has given rise to numerous instances where individuals find themselves entangled with the police for expressing views that someone else deemed offensive.

For example, in 2019, a man was investigated by the police for retweeting a joke about transgender identity. Though no charges were filed, the police visited him at home, warning him to be mindful of his social media activity. This case is far from isolated. Other examples include people being arrested for jokes, tweets, or even casual comments that were reported as offensive. The Orwellian overtones are unmistakable here: the state, through these "non-criminal hate incidents," is monitoring and regulating not only actions but also thoughts and opinions that fall outside of the socially accepted framework.

These incidents serve as a potent reminder that Orwell's *1984* is not just a work of fiction. The notion of *Big Brother* an omnipresent surveillance state that seeks to control the population by regulating thought and speech has a modern-day corollary in the UK's hate speech enforcement apparatus. Although these measures are framed as being in the public interest, the result is a climate where individuals must constantly weigh the potential legal repercussions of expressing their beliefs.

Social Media Regulation: The New Public Square

In addition to these legal instruments, the UK has also taken steps to regulate online speech, particularly on social media platforms. Social media has, in many ways, become the new public square, where ideas are exchanged, debated, and contested. However, it has also become a space where speech is policed more heavily than ever before. The Online Safety Bill, which has been making its way through Parliament, is a case in point. Its proponents argue that the bill is necessary to combat online harassment, misinformation, and extremist content, but its critics warn that it will have a chilling effect on free expression.

The bill empowers regulatory bodies like Ofcom to monitor and penalize platforms that fail to remove harmful content. Yet, defining what constitutes "harmful" content is a notoriously difficult task. Much like the public order laws and hate speech regulations, the bill's vague language creates an environment where platforms may err on the side of caution and remove content that is merely controversial or unpopular, rather than genuinely harmful. As seen in the United States, where social media companies act as de facto gatekeepers of speech (Chapter 2), the UK's approach risks further entrenching this trend.

Synopsis of the Public Order Bill and Its Implications

The Public Order Bill, passed by the UK Parliament on April 27, 2023, has raised significant concerns regarding its compatibility with international human rights obligations, particularly regarding the right to freedom of expression, peaceful assembly, and association. UN High Commissioner for Human Rights, Volker Türk, expressed alarm, warning that the law imposes unnecessary and disproportionate restrictions on these rights.

Key elements of the bill include expanded powers for the police to conduct stop-and-search operations without suspicion, vague definitions of new criminal offences, and the introduction of Serious Disruption Prevention Orders (SDPOs). These orders can limit individuals' movements, associations, or use of the internet and may apply even to those who have not been convicted of a crime. This raises concerns about pre-emptive restrictions on peaceful protests, especially those related to human rights and environmental issues. Türk emphasized that while governments have to maintain public order, they must also facilitate peaceful protests. The bill, he argued, undermines the UK's long-standing commitment to human rights and should be reversed.

The Labour Government's Use of the Public Order Bill to Suppress Dissent

Since becoming Prime Minister, Sir Keir Starmer has faced scrutiny for his handling of civil liberties under the Public Order Bill. While the legislation was introduced under a Conservative government, Starmer's Labour Party has not repealed or strongly opposed its implementation. Critics argue that the Labour government is leveraging the bill to stifle dissent, particularly from environmental and social justice movements, which often employ non-violent but disruptive protest tactics.

The law's vague definitions of "serious disruption" and its potential use against individuals without prior convictions have raised fears that it could be wielded to suppress political opposition. By enabling pre-emptive measures, such as SDPOs, the government can limit activists' ability to organize or participate in protests, thereby quashing dissent before it materializes. The expanded stop-and-search powers further exacerbate concerns about the disproportionate targeting of marginalized groups and activists.

In this context, Starmer's government is perceived as continuing or even intensifying a legislative framework that curbs civil liberties, particularly those related to protest movements. This has sparked criticisms from human rights groups, who see it as a worrying trend toward authoritarianism, curbing legitimate democratic expressions of opposition and dissent.

This development is particularly troubling when we consider the role of social media in modern political discourse. When individuals face the possibility of legal consequences for their online activity, they may self-censor or avoid engaging in discussions that challenge the status quo. This "chilling effect" stifles the kind of open debate that is essential to a healthy democracy. Once again, Orwell's *1984* offers a prescient warning: by narrowing the range of permissible thought, the state can effectively control the population, not through brute force, but through the quiet suppression of dissent.

The Pressure to Conform: A Cultural Shift

It is important to note that the chilling effects of public order laws and hate speech regulations are not solely the result of government actions. There has been a broader cultural shift in the UK, where social norms and expectations increasingly pressure individuals to conform to certain viewpoints. Those who express opinions that deviate from mainstream ideologies risk being ostracized, "cancelled," or even subjected to legal consequences. This cultural climate, where dissent is discouraged, complements the legal restrictions already in place.

As I highlighted in the previous chapter on Canada, Orwell's *Animal Farm* provides a useful framework for understanding how well-meaning policies can evolve into authoritarian controls. What begins as a movement for equality can quickly morph into a mechanism for suppressing free speech. In the UK, the goal of protecting marginalized groups from harm is laudable, but it has led to a situation where the mere expression of dissenting views is seen as inherently harmful. The line between protection and control becomes increasingly blurred.

Conclusion: The Erosion of Free Speech in the UK

The UK's public order laws hate speech regulations, and efforts to police online discourse have created an environment where free speech is under threat. While these measures are often justified in the name of public safety or social harmony, their cumulative effect has been to silence dissent and discourage open debate. The parallels to Orwell's dystopian visions are hard to ignore. As we move forward, the question remains: will the UK be able to balance the protection of vulnerable groups with the preservation of free speech, or will it continue down the path toward an increasingly controlled and conformist society? In exploring these dynamics, it becomes clear that the very freedoms once taken for granted are now being systematically eroded, often in the name of protecting the public from harm.

Chapter 5: Europe – Balancing Tolerance and Free Expression

In the ever-evolving landscape of European politics and social values, few issues strike at the heart of democratic societies quite like the tension between tolerance and free expression. On the one hand, there is a shared European commitment to protecting individuals and communities from harm, particularly from hate speech, disinformation, and the abuses of modern digital platforms. On the other, there is the bedrock principle of free speech, which for centuries has been a hallmark of European democratic governance. In this chapter, I will explore how countries such as Germany, France, and the Netherlands have navigated this delicate balance. We will examine how laws intended to preserve social harmony, though well-meaning, have sometimes led to overreach, stifling legitimate discourse in the process.

Germany – A History Shaped by the Past

Germany's approach to free speech is profoundly shaped by its historical legacy. Given its experience with totalitarianism in the 20th century, particularly the horrors of the Nazi regime, the German state has been vigilant about preventing the resurgence of extremism. This has resulted in some of the most stringent hate speech laws in Europe. Under Germany's *Strafgesetzbuch* (Criminal Code), for example, Holocaust denial is not only considered hate speech but is also criminalised, as is the use of Nazi symbols and the incitement of racial hatred. While these measures have been largely applauded for fostering social peace and preventing far-right extremism from gaining a foothold, they have also ignited debate over the boundaries of free expression.

One particularly notable piece of legislation is the Network Enforcement Act, or *NetzDG*, which came into effect in 2017. This law compels social media platforms to remove "obviously illegal" content, including hate speech and defamation, within 24 hours or face hefty fines. Ostensibly, the *NetzDG* seeks to protect public discourse from harmful content, but critics argue that its vague definitions and tight deadlines create a chilling effect. Many fear that social media companies, eager to avoid fines, may over-censor, removing content that falls within the scope of legitimate political debate.

Here, we see shades of Orwell's concept of "thoughtcrime" from *1984*, where dissenting thoughts themselves become criminal. While Germany aims to avoid a return to the totalitarian ideologies of its past, the unintended consequence is that public debate is increasingly shaped by fear of legal repercussions, restricting the diversity of opinion necessary for a healthy democracy.

France – Liberté, Egalité, Contradiction

France, too, grapples with the balance between free expression and the protection of social order, particularly in a society deeply committed to the principles of *liberté, égalité, fraternité*. However, the French experience is marked by its unique challenges, not least of which is the tension between secularism (*laïcité*) and religious expression. France has enacted robust hate speech laws, codified in the *Loi sur la presse de 1881*, which prohibits speech that incites hatred, discrimination, or violence based on race, religion, or sexual orientation.

However, France's approach to managing public discourse is far from uniform. The infamous *Charlie Hebdo* affair is perhaps the most dramatic example of the country's complex relationship with free speech. In the wake of the attacks on the satirical magazine, French society rallied around the notion of free expression, with millions declaring "Je suis Charlie" as a symbol of defiance. Yet, in the years since France has paradoxically tightened speech laws. In 2020, the so-called "Avia Law," aimed at combating online hate, was introduced. Although key provisions were later struck down by the Constitutional Council, the legislation proposed to compel online platforms to remove hate speech within 24 hours, eerily like Germany's *NetzDG*.

Here, again, we encounter the Orwellian dilemma. In France, the defence of secularism and social cohesion has at times veered into an overzealous policing of thought. Critics argue that laws intended to protect society from hate have also been weaponised to silence dissent, particularly around contentious issues like immigration, race relations, and religious identity. The spectre of "thoughtcrime" looms large in a society increasingly divided between its ideals of absolute freedom and the demands of an evolving, multicultural reality.

The Netherlands – A Tradition of Tolerance Under Strain

The Netherlands has long prided itself on its tradition of tolerance, a nation where free speech is cherished, and differences of opinion are not just accepted but encouraged. Yet even here, the balance between tolerance and free expression is becoming harder to maintain. Dutch law prohibits incitement to hatred or violence based on race, religion, or sexual orientation, and notable cases, such as the trial of Geert Wilders for his inflammatory anti-Islam rhetoric, have tested the limits of this principle.

Wilders, a far-right politician, has often pushed the boundaries of what is acceptable in public discourse, making highly controversial statements that many view as hate speech. His legal battles underscore a growing challenge in Europe: how to handle populist voices that tap into societal fears and prejudices while preserving the core values of free expression. The courts have, in some cases, sided with free speech, but not without significant public outcry. The Netherlands exemplifies a Europe that is increasingly divided between maintaining an open forum for debate and the pressing need to safeguard vulnerable groups from harm.

The European Union – Regulating the Digital Public Square

At the supranational level, the European Union has taken a proactive role in regulating speech, particularly in the digital realm. The EU's Digital Services Act (DSA), which seeks to create a safer online environment, has far-reaching implications for free expression across the continent. The DSA obliges platforms to remove illegal content more efficiently and imposes transparency measures regarding content moderation decisions. While the act is aimed at curbing hate speech, disinformation, and terrorist propaganda online, it has been criticized for encouraging over-regulation by tech companies, leading to the risk of lawful speech being removed in the process.

The DSA reflects a broader European trend: a well-intentioned effort to combat the worst excesses of online speech often ends up stifling more than just hate. Orwell's warning in *1984* about the consequences of controlling thought through language is more relevant than ever. With digital platforms now the primary venue for public discourse, the line between legitimate moderation and censorship is becoming increasingly blurred. In many ways, the DSA represents the culmination of Europe's struggle to balance tolerance with freedom a balancing act that risks tipping towards the suppression of dissenting voices.

The EU Digital Services Act (DSA), which became fully applicable on 17 February 2024, introduces a wide-ranging legal framework aimed at enhancing the accountability of online intermediaries and platforms (such as online marketplaces, social networks, and content-sharing platforms) operating within Europe. Its core objective is to prevent illegal and harmful activities, reduce the spread of disinformation, and protect users from unsafe online practices. To achieve this, the DSA imposes strict obligations regarding transparency, content moderation, and dispute resolution.

However, the DSA's impact on free speech has raised concerns, as some of its provisions, if misused or misapplied, could have a chilling effect on open expression across the EU's digital landscape.

Key Provisions with Potential Chilling Effects:

- **Content Moderation and Reporting**: The DSA mandates that platforms introduce mechanisms for reporting illegal content and ensuring its swift removal. While this is designed to protect users, there is a risk that platforms may overzealously censor legitimate content to avoid penalties. Over-moderation could suppress political discourse, artistic expression, and criticism, especially when navigating the fine line between harmful speech and free speech.

- **Transparency in Targeted Advertisements and AI**: Platforms must provide transparency when using AI algorithms and targeted advertising. While this improves user awareness, the pressure on platforms to comply with complex rules may lead to automated systems that indiscriminately flag or remove content without nuanced consideration of context, thereby limiting free expression.

- **Dispute Resolution and Accountability**: While the DSA provides mechanisms for resolving disputes between users and platforms, it may also create an environment where platforms are incentivized to err on the side of caution. Fear of liability could drive platforms to pre-emptively remove contentious or politically sensitive content, even if it does not violate any laws. This could disproportionately affect minority viewpoints or controversial opinions, effectively silencing important voices in public debate.

Consequences for Free Speech:

1. **Over-Censorship**: The DSA's broad mandate to remove harmful or illegal content could lead to over-censorship by platforms, either through algorithmic errors or excessive caution. This could curtail discussions on sensitive but critical issues, such as political dissent, social justice, and emerging scientific debates, stifling freedom of expression in the process.
2. **Suppression of Minority Voices**: Smaller platforms or emerging companies, lacking resources to implement

sophisticated moderation mechanisms, may be more inclined to remove content pre-emptively. This could disproportionately affect marginalized groups or dissident voices, who rely on these platforms to share alternative viewpoints and challenge mainstream narratives.

3. **Impact on Journalism and Whistleblowing**: Journalistic investigations or whistleblowing efforts, which often tread the line between legality and public interest, may be particularly vulnerable under the DSA. Content exposing corruption, governmental misconduct, or corporate malfeasance could be flagged as harmful or illegal, leading to its removal before public scrutiny can occur.

4. **Automated Censorship by AI**: As platforms scale up content moderation through AI, there is a significant risk of mistakes in interpretation. Automated systems may struggle to understand satire, irony, or political speech, leading to the inadvertent silencing of legitimate content. The nuance required for healthy democratic debate may be lost in the rigidity of automated moderation.

5. **Chilling Effect on Platforms and Creators**: The fear of non-compliance, fines, or legal action may push platforms to adopt overly restrictive policies, limiting what users can post and share. This cautious approach, while protective against illegal content, could chill free expression, as creators, journalists, and users self-censor out of fear of breaching the DSA's provisions.

Overall Impact:

While the DSA is intended to safeguard users from harmful and illegal activities online, its rigid requirements and the heavy burden placed on platforms to police content could inadvertently stifle free speech. The potential for overreach, over-censorship, and the silencing of minority voices could undermine open discourse and democratic dialogue across Europe. If not carefully balanced, the DSA's measures could have a chilling effect on the very freedoms it aims to protect, reducing the diversity of voices in Europe's digital public sphere.

Conclusion: A Delicate Balance at Risk

As we have seen in this chapter, European countries have embraced a wide range of approaches to managing speech. While each nation has its own cultural and historical reasons for pursuing stringent hate speech laws, the overarching trend is one of growing intervention in the realm of public discourse. This intervention is often well-meaning, grounded in the need to protect society from the dangers of hatred, disinformation, and extremism. Yet, as we have explored in previous chapters whether in the United Kingdom, Canada, or the United States the attempt to regulate speech often comes at a cost.

In Europe, the cost may well be the erosion of one of its most prized democratic values: the ability to speak freely without fear of legal retribution. The chilling effect of hate speech laws, combined with the increasing control of digital platforms under regulations like the Digital Services Act, is creating an environment in which dissent is not just discouraged but criminalised. As Orwell presciently warned, once the boundaries of acceptable thought are defined by the state, we risk entering a world where freedom exists only in name, not in practice.

In the next chapter, we shall turn our attention to Australia, a nation whose own balance between free expression and regulation is evolving in response to both domestic and global pressures, providing yet another lens through which we can examine the gradual erosion of speech rights across Western democracies.

Chapter 6: Australia – Free Speech vs. Harm Minimisation

Australia presents a compelling case when discussing the global erosion of free speech in the name of public welfare. While often celebrated as a vibrant democracy, the country's legal framework for protecting free speech is not as robust as one might expect when compared to other Western democracies such as the United States or even the United Kingdom. As we have seen in **Chapter 5**, Europe has leaned towards balancing tolerance and free expression, but Australia's approach is distinct. The nation has embraced a legislative model that leans heavily towards *harm minimisation*, frequently at the expense of individual liberties.

At the heart of this issue is the tension between free speech and the increasing regulation of public discourse, particularly online. Australia's anti-discrimination laws, media regulations, and the use of social media censorship have all come under scrutiny, raising the question: when does the protection of the public from harm become indistinguishable from the suppression of dissent?

Anti-Discrimination Laws and the 'Greater Good'

Australia's anti-discrimination framework is well-intentioned and aimed at creating an inclusive society where individuals are protected from harmful speech, particularly on grounds of race, gender, and religion. Yet, as has been discussed in earlier chapters on **Canada (Chapter 3)** and **the United Kingdom (Chapter 4)**, legislation of this kind can often venture into overreach. The **Racial Discrimination Act of 1975**, particularly Section 18C, exemplifies this challenge. Introduced to curb racial vilification, the provision prohibits any act that is "reasonably likely, in all the circumstances, to offend, insult, humiliate or intimidate another person or a group of people" based on race or ethnicity.

While this law was created with good intentions, it has become a flashpoint in the debate over the limits of free speech in Australia. Detractors argue that the wording of Section 18C is overly broad and has been used as a tool to stifle legitimate debate. This is evident in high-profile cases such as the **Andrew Bolt case in 2011**, where the controversial columnist was found guilty of breaching 18C for articles questioning the legitimacy of certain individuals identifying as Indigenous. The ruling, in this case, prompted widespread debate about whether Australia was heading down the slippery slope of restricting speech that offends but may still serve as valuable social commentary.

The use of anti-discrimination laws to protect individuals from harm, though noble, has led to a climate where robust debate is chilled. Those who question established narratives whether on race, gender, or social issues are often met with legal challenges or public vilification. It is here that we see the echoes of **Orwell's Animal Farm**, where dissenting opinions are suppressed not by direct force, but by appeals to the collective good. The justification is always the same: it is for the welfare of all, and yet, it is the dissenters who suffer the greatest harm. Much like the silencing of the animals who challenge the pigs' authority in *Animal Farm*, Australian dissenters are increasingly marginalised under the guise of promoting social harmony.

Regulating the Media: The Fourth Estate Under Siege

Australia's media landscape has also seen increasing regulation, with the government and independent bodies taking steps to control what can and cannot be said in both traditional and digital media. One recent legislative effort, the **News Media Bargaining Code**, sought to compel tech giants like Facebook and Google to pay news organisations for content shared on their platforms. While ostensibly designed to protect journalism and ensure a free and diverse press, it inadvertently demonstrated how easily the government could intervene in the flow of information.

The **Australian Communications and Media Authority (ACMA)** has gained increasing power to oversee media conduct and regulate content deemed harmful or offensive. This trend aligns with what we observed in **Chapter 4** regarding the UK's public order laws. Australian public discourse is becoming more policed, not just by the government but by private platforms and media outlets wary of being penalised for the content they host.

The rise of **social media censorship** in Australia adds a new layer to the regulatory landscape. Platforms like Facebook and Twitter have adopted stringent content moderation policies under pressure from both public opinion and government initiatives. In 2019, following the Christchurch shooting in New Zealand, Australia passed the **Sharing of Abhorrent Violent Material Act**, which imposed severe penalties on social media companies that fail to quickly remove violent content. While motivated by a tragic event, this law again underscores the risks associated with hastily implemented speech restrictions. The line between protecting the public from harm and eroding free speech has become blurred.

Social media platforms, seeking to comply with these regulations, have adopted aggressive censorship strategies, often silencing not only dangerous content but also dissenting voices that challenge mainstream views. This mirrors the concept of **thoughtcrime** from Orwell's *1984*, discussed in **Chapter 5** concerning Europe's hate speech laws. Increasingly, online platforms are acting as arbiters of acceptable speech, deleting content or suspending users who step outside the bounds of what is deemed appropriate. As the Australian government tightens its grip on digital discourse, it raises the question: how much freedom are we willing to sacrifice for the sake of harm minimisation?

Political Correctness in Academia: The New Orthodoxy

The rise of **political correctness** in Australian universities and public institutions is another worrying trend. As with many Western countries, Australia has seen a shift in academic culture where open debate is replaced with rigid orthodoxy. Universities, once bastions of free thought, are now becoming environments where certain opinions are not only discouraged but actively suppressed.

In a 2020 study by the **Institute of Public Affairs**, it was found that **over 80% of Australian universities had policies that restricted free speech**. Speech codes, 'safe spaces,' and the de-platforming of controversial speakers have become commonplace. These institutions justify such measures in the name of protecting students from harm, yet the result is the stifling of intellectual diversity. Students and professors alike are afraid to express unpopular opinions for fear of professional repercussions or social ostracism.

This new orthodoxy is starkly reminiscent of the social dynamics in *Animal Farm*, where dissenting animals are silenced to maintain the illusion of equality and progress. In the same way that Orwell's animals found themselves under the heel of the pigs, students and academics are finding themselves increasingly constrained by the pressures of political correctness. What was once a space for intellectual exploration has become an echo chamber, where only the most sanitised, socially acceptable ideas can thrive.

Conclusion: The Erosion of Australian Discourse

Australia's approach to free speech, with its emphasis on harm minimisation, reflects a growing trend seen throughout the Western world, as discussed in previous chapters. In balancing the protection of marginalised groups and maintaining social harmony, the nation has adopted an increasingly restrictive stance on what can be said in public, online, and in academic spaces. The tension between safeguarding individuals from harm and preserving the right to dissent is becoming untenable.

Orwell's *Animal Farm* offers a poignant metaphor for the situation in Australia. The justification for speech restrictions is always framed as serving the 'greater good', much like the pigs in the novel claiming their authority was necessary for the benefit of all animals. Yet, as Orwell reminds us when speech is controlled for the sake of the many, it is often the few who suffer the greatest loss.

The road Australia is treading, as we have seen in **Chapters 2 through 5**, mirrors a broader global trend of eroding free speech rights under the guise of protection. As Australians grapple with the tension between free speech and harm minimisation, one cannot help but wonder whether the country will continue down this path or find a way to reclaim its commitment to open discourse. The erosion may be subtle, but its echoes are unmistakably Orwellian.

Chapter 7: Technology and the Digital Landscape – Modern-Day Thought Police

As I delve into the realm of the digital landscape, I cannot help but draw stark parallels between the omnipresent surveillance and manipulation in George Orwell's *1984* and the modern-day practices of our tech giants. The contemporary world is one where governments, corporations, and particularly technology companies hold vast influence over the scope of free speech. The mechanisms through which these entities operate resemble, in many ways, the *thought police* not as literal enforcers, but as gatekeepers who determine what can be said, what can be seen, and ultimately, what can be thought. This chapter will explore how these tech conglomerates Facebook, Twitter (now X), and Google, among others act as digital custodians of speech, subtly and overtly regulating discourse in ways that eerily mirror Orwell's dystopian vision.

The Intersection of Governments, Corporations, and Technology

To begin, the collaboration between governments and tech companies in monitoring and regulating speech has become increasingly conspicuous. It is no secret that, in the aftermath of events like the Arab Spring, elections, and even the COVID-19 pandemic, governments have sought to exert control over the dissemination of information. They have enlisted tech giants as their de facto enforcers, encouraging or at times coercing them to remove content deemed harmful or misleading. While the initial intention behind these efforts may have been well-meaning, aimed at preserving social stability or public health, they have given rise to a pervasive form of censorship that limits genuine dissent and debate.

Governments have found tech companies a ready ally, as these corporations have a vested interest in maintaining a certain level of public order. But unlike traditional government censorship, which has clear boundaries, the algorithms and policies developed by these tech giants operate in an opaque and often unchallengeable manner. In this sense, the role of corporations in shaping and restricting speech has expanded beyond merely complying with government mandates; they have taken on a life of their own as arbiters of acceptable discourse.

De-platforming and Shadow Banning: The Quiet Silencing of Dissent.

One of the most visible manifestations of this control is the practice of de-platforming. Public figures, activists, and commentators who hold views that diverge from mainstream narratives are often removed from platforms like Twitter or YouTube without clear justification or recourse. In previous chapters, such as Chapter 2, where I explored the United States' First Amendment challenges, we see how this practice is often framed as necessary to combat hate speech or disinformation. However, de-platforming has become a tool that stretches beyond combating extremism; it is now regularly wielded against individuals who express unpopular or contrarian opinions on contentious topics such as politics, gender identity, or public health.

Shadow banning, a more insidious practice, deserves special attention. Unlike de-platforming, where a user's presence is outright removed, shadow banning is a covert form of suppression. Here, the user remains on the platform, unaware that their posts are being suppressed, seen by only a fraction of their audience. It is a modern form of Orwellian doublethink: the user believes they are participating in the marketplace of ideas, while their voice has been quietly muted. What is particularly troubling is the lack of transparency in these processes. Algorithms, developed in corporate boardrooms and operating without public oversight, decide whose voices are heard and whose are silenced. As discussed in Chapter 6 on Australia, where media regulation has blurred the lines of free speech and harm minimisation, we find that the very tools designed to connect and inform us are being weaponised against dissenters.

The Algorithmic Manipulation of Discourse

Algorithms are the unseen architects of our digital experience. They curate the content we see, subtly guiding our opinions by presenting us with information deemed acceptable by opaque corporate standards. Much like the "telescreens" of Orwell's *1984*, which constantly broadcast state propaganda, the algorithms of platforms like Facebook, Google, and Twitter ensure that users are fed a stream of information that reinforces pre-approved narratives. While this might not always be intentional, the result is a narrowing of permissible viewpoints, a filter bubble where only certain ideas thrive.

What makes this algorithmic control particularly dangerous is its ability to shape public discourse without the public's conscious awareness. In Chapter 5, we examined Europe's attempts to balance tolerance with free speech, often at the cost of stifling dissent through regulations. In the digital realm, this control is far more pervasive and subtle. Users often assume they are seeing a diverse range of opinions, yet their feeds are shaped by algorithms designed to prioritise engagement over truth, and sensationalism over nuance. What is promoted is often what serves the interests of the platform, be that advertising revenue or compliance with regulatory bodies. The algorithms, in effect, become the modern thought police, deciding which ideas deserve amplification and which should be hidden away in the shadows.

Orwell's *1984* and the Concept of "Thoughtcrime"

Orwell's depiction of *thoughtcrime* the notion that even thinking against the regime is punishable bears a chilling resemblance to how digital platforms now treat certain viewpoints. While we are not yet at a point where our thoughts are monitored, the line between thought and expression has become perilously thin. In Chapter 4, we examined the UK's use of public order laws to police speech, even going so far as to criminalise casual remarks on social media. On digital platforms, controversial ideas are often met not with reasoned debate but with algorithmic suppression or outright removal, as if merely voicing dissent constitutes a crime against the established order.

Tech companies have adopted the role of judge, jury, and executioner. Whether it's through their content moderation policies or their collaborations with governments, they have positioned themselves as the final arbiters of truth in the digital space. This is not unlike the Ministry of Truth in *1984*, which rewrote history and controlled all knowledge. The algorithms and content moderation policies employed today serve a similar purpose they edit the narrative, exclude opposing viewpoints, and rewrite the truth in real time, all under the guise of protecting the public from harm.

Conclusion: The Silent March Towards Digital Authoritarianism

What emerges from this exploration is a stark realisation: we are living in an age where the boundaries of acceptable speech are not set by governments alone but by unelected tech corporations. These companies, through their algorithms and moderation policies, have become the custodians of public discourse, and in doing so, have taken on the role of Orwell's *thought police*. The de-platforming of individuals, shadow banning of dissent, and algorithmic manipulation of content all point to a digital authoritarianism that suppresses dissent without the need for overt government censorship.

The rise of this digital landscape, as discussed in previous chapters, has created an environment where speech is regulated not by laws alone but by the unseen hand of technology. We are being conditioned to self-censor, to conform to the narrow bounds of acceptable thought set by an invisible algorithm. In the end, it is not just governments but the very platforms we rely on for communication and knowledge that are eroding our freedom of speech. The digital landscape, it seems, has become the stage upon which the battle for free expression will be fought and unless we are vigilant, it is a battle we may already be losing.

Chapter 8: The Role of Academia – Indoctrination or Education?

In the tapestry of democratic societies, universities have long held the mantle of being incubators of critical thought, fostering an environment where ideas however controversial can be tested, debated, and refined. At their best, these institutions are pillars of intellectual freedom, ensuring the continuation of a tradition where knowledge is not merely handed down but rigorously examined. Yet, in recent decades, these same institutions have increasingly found themselves at the centre of a troubling paradox: while they are meant to be bastions of free thought, many have come under scrutiny for stifling dissenting voices, especially those that challenge the dominant ideological paradigms on campus.

The question at the heart of this chapter is whether academia has shifted from education to indoctrination, particularly through the promotion of left-leaning ideologies that discourage open debate. To be clear, this critique is not about political bias *per se*, bias, after all, is an inevitable part of human thought, but rather about how certain ideological frameworks have become entrenched within the academic world, often to the detriment of the free exchange of ideas. This issue, already touched upon in earlier chapters, reflects broader societal trends (as seen in **Chapter 4** in the United Kingdom, where public order laws are used to suppress offensive speech), but academia represents a unique battleground in this ongoing struggle.

Universities have always been political in some sense. However, the current climate on many campuses suggests that we have entered a new phase, one in which certain ideologies particularly those tied to critical theory, intersectionality, and identity politics are not merely present but dominate the discourse, often to the exclusion of competing viewpoints. It is here that we begin to see the worrying parallels with Orwell's *Animal*

Farm, where the rhetoric of equality is gradually transformed into a tool for social control.

The Rise of Critical Theory and Intersectionality

Critical theory, originating in the Frankfurt School of the early 20th century, has long been a tool for analysing power structures within society. While it once served as a valuable lens through which to critique dominant ideologies, particularly in capitalist societies, it has morphed over time. Today, critical theory along with its offshoot, intersectionality forms the backbone of much contemporary academic discourse, particularly in the humanities and social sciences. These frameworks are often presented as neutral or objective tools for understanding the world, but in practice, they can foster a particular worldview that is resistant to challenge.

Intersectionality has gained significant traction as a framework for understanding how various forms of oppression (such as racism, sexism, and homophobia) overlap and interact. While there is merit in analysing the complex ways in which different identities intersect, this framework can also lead to a rigid hierarchy of victimhood, where the legitimacy of one's viewpoint is determined by their perceived position within that hierarchy. This can stifle genuine debate, as those deemed to be in privileged positions are often dismissed or silenced outright. In essence, this form of argumentation by prioritising lived experience over rational discourse can act as a form of censorship, where certain voices are deemed unworthy of being heard, a theme that Orwell would likely recognise as an echo of *Animal Farm*'s famous proclamation: *"All animals are equal, but some animals are more equal than others."*

Safe Spaces and Speech Codes: Protecting or Policing Thought?

One of the more visible manifestations of this ideological shift within academia has been the proliferation of "safe spaces" and the introduction of speech codes aimed at fostering inclusivity. The intention behind these measures is, ostensibly, a noble one: to create environments where students from marginalised backgrounds feel secure and supported. However, the unintended consequence or perhaps the intended one, depending on one's viewpoint has been the creation of intellectual echo chambers, where certain ideas are protected from criticism and dissenting viewpoints are either marginalised or outright banned.

The concept of safe spaces, while well-meaning, can quickly devolve into a form of intellectual protectionism, where students are shielded from ideas that challenge their worldviews. This is not merely an academic concern; it has profound implications for the very purpose of education. If universities become places where only certain viewpoints are tolerated, then we are not educating students to think critically but rather indoctrinating them into a particular ideological framework. The introduction of speech codes, which often go together with safe spaces, only exacerbates this problem. Under the guise of promoting inclusivity, these codes frequently restrict speech that is deemed offensive or harmful, effectively policing thought in a way that Orwell would have found deeply troubling.

In **Chapter** 7, we discussed the role of technology in shaping the boundaries of acceptable discourse, with tech companies acting as modern-day thought police. The parallels in academia are striking. Just as social media platforms use algorithms to suppress dissenting voices, universities have increasingly relied on bureaucratic mechanisms such as bias response teams and mandatory diversity training to ensure conformity to the prevailing orthodoxy. In both cases, the result is a narrowing of the space for genuine debate, where individuals are encouraged to self-censor for fear of social or professional repercussions.

The Perils of Identity Politics

Perhaps nowhere is this ideological conformity more evident than in the rise of identity politics on campus. While the original aim of identity politics was to draw attention to the unique experiences of marginalised groups, it has since evolved into a tool for dividing people along racial, gender, and sexual lines. Rather than fostering an environment where individuals are judged by the content of their character or the quality of their ideas, identity politics encourages students to see themselves and others primarily through the lens of group identity.

This is problematic for several reasons. First, it reinforces the notion that individuals are defined primarily by their immutable characteristics, rather than their actions or beliefs. Second, it creates a culture of victimhood, where the focus is on grievance rather than dialogue. Third, it fosters an environment where disagreement is interpreted as an attack on one's identity, rather than a legitimate difference of opinion. This not only stifles debate but also erodes the very foundations of liberal democracy, which depend on the ability of individuals to engage with each other as equals in the marketplace of ideas.

In **Chapter 6**, we saw how Australia's harm minimisation approach to free speech has led to a culture where dissent is increasingly suppressed in the name of protecting marginalised groups. The same dynamic is at play within academia, where the desire to protect students from harm whether real or perceived often leads to the silencing of those who challenge the dominant ideological narratives. In both cases, the rhetoric of inclusion is used to justify censorship, echoing Orwell's warning in *Animal Farm* about how ideals can be perverted to serve the interests of those in power.

Conclusion: Academia at a Crossroads

The role of academia in shaping the future of free speech cannot be overstated. Universities have always been the crucible in which new ideas are forged, tested, and either refined or discarded. Yet, if current trends continue, we risk transforming our universities from places of learning into factories of conformity, where students are not encouraged to think critically but rather taught what to think. The rise of critical theory, intersectionality, and identity politics combined with the proliferation of safe spaces and speech codes represents a serious challenge to the ideal of free expression within academia.

If we are to preserve the spirit of intellectual inquiry that has long defined our universities, we must be willing to confront these trends head-on. This will require a recommitment to the principles of open debate and the free exchange of ideas, even when those ideas are uncomfortable or controversial. As Orwell reminds us in *Animal Farm*, the rhetoric of equality can easily be twisted into a tool for control, and if we are not vigilant, the same fate may await our universities.

Chapter 9: Resistance and Backlash – Fighting for Free Speech

The tightening grip on free speech that we explored in earlier chapters has not gone uncontested. In this chapter, I turn to the growing resistance against these incursions, examining how diverse groups ranging from grassroots movements to civil libertarians and political figures have mobilized to counter the creeping tide of censorship. These voices of defiance echo Orwell's observation in *1984* of the proles, those often-overlooked masses who, despite being neglected by the ruling elite, held the latent power to rebel against the system.

To appreciate the scale of this backlash, we must first understand the root of the discontent. As detailed in Chapter 7, the role of tech companies in policing online discourse has become a focal point of resistance. People have grown increasingly aware that these platforms, once heralded as spaces for open dialogue, have morphed into the gatekeepers of expression. This realisation has given rise to a series of legal battles, with individuals and organisations suing tech giants for their de-platforming practices, accusing them of suppressing dissent in the name of "community standards" or "terms of service." A notable example is the case of **Alex Berenson**, a journalist who took legal action after being banned from Twitter (now X) for questioning the mainstream narrative on COVID-19 policies. His lawsuit, which led to a temporary reinstatement, exemplifies how figures from across the political spectrum are pushing back through legal means.

Similarly, grassroots movements have begun to challenge the broader culture of censorship. One of the most prominent groups to emerge in recent years is **The Free Speech Union**, an organisation dedicated to defending individuals from punitive actions taken against them for expressing controversial opinions. The Union's advocacy cuts across political lines, underscoring the non-partisan nature of free speech defence. Their campaigns have successfully raised public awareness about the quiet silencing of voices, often under the guise of preventing harm or protecting vulnerable groups, as we discussed in Chapter 6 regarding Australia's harm minimisation laws.

What is most compelling about this resistance is the coalition of unlikely allies it has forged. Traditional conservatives, often critical of progressive ideology, have joined forces with classical liberals and civil libertarians who view the suppression of free speech as an existential threat to democracy itself. This is particularly evident in the United States, where lawsuits have emerged against both government policies and corporate censorship, as highlighted in Chapter 2. In a striking parallel to Orwell's *1984*, these movements frequently refer to the notion of "doublethink," accusing governments and institutions of weaponising language to control thought. Terms like "misinformation," "hate speech," and "disinformation" are often employed not as objective descriptors but as tools to quash opposition. In response, lawsuits have been filed against governmental overreach, including challenges to the **Communications Decency Act's Section 230**, which grants broad immunity to tech platforms while allowing them to censor user-generated content with little accountability.

These lawsuits and movements serve as a vital counterweight to the growing acceptance of censorship in the public sphere, particularly in academia, as covered in Chapter 8. Universities, once the bastions of intellectual freedom, have become battlegrounds where the very principles of free expression are at stake. Resistance has also emerged within these institutions, most visibly through the actions of students, professors, and intellectuals who have refused to bow to ideological orthodoxy. Individuals like **Bret Weinstein** a biology professor at Evergreen State College became the focal point of national attention when he was driven out of the institution for refusing to comply with race-based "day of absence" policies. Weinstein's story, widely publicised, stands as a chilling reminder of how even the mildest dissent can be punished in today's academic environments, which increasingly resemble the thought-controlled spaces of Orwell's *Animal Farm*.

Orwell's portrayal of the proles as a largely passive group, ignored by the Party, bears an unsettling resemblance to how many modern governments view the general population—seen more as subjects to be managed than as active participants in democratic discourse. Yet in *1984*, Orwell hints at the potential for the proles to awaken and rise, though they remain largely dormant within the narrative. Today's dissenters are analogous to these proles, representing a vast, untapped potential for meaningful resistance against the encroachments on free speech. The question is whether this potential will be fully realised before it's too late.

Political movements, particularly those on the right, have increasingly positioned themselves as defenders of free speech. Figures such as **Ron DeSantis** in the United States and **Nigel Farage** in the UK have capitalised on the frustrations of those who feel stifled by political correctness and cancel culture. DeSantis, for instance, has spearheaded legislation in Florida that aims to curb what he and his supporters see as the ideological censorship of conservative voices in education and online. Farage, on the other hand, has become a vocal critic of the UK's public order laws, which we analysed in Chapter 4, particularly in how these laws are used to police speech deemed "offensive" or "hate-filled." The common thread between these movements is their emphasis on the right to offend, a right they argue is indispensable to a truly free society.

Moreover, there is a notable resurgence in the appeal to classical liberal principles, especially within the legal realm. Organisations such as **The American Civil Liberties Union (ACLU)**, historically a left-leaning institution, have faced internal rifts over their traditional commitment to defending free speech, even for those with whom they disagree politically. Yet there remains a strong contingent within the ACLU and similar organisations that recognise the danger of allowing governments or private corporations to determine the boundaries of acceptable discourse. This faction continues to fight, often at great personal and professional cost, for the idea that free speech must include the freedom to express uncomfortable or even abhorrent ideas.

In some instances, resistance takes on a more cultural dimension, as artists, comedians, and commentators push back against the censorious atmosphere by directly challenging the taboos of the day. Figures like **Ricky Gervais**, who frequently mocks the sacred cows of modern political discourse in his stand-up routines, exemplify how comedy and satire remain powerful tools in the fight for free expression. Gervais and others recognise that the moment certain ideas are placed beyond criticism, the foundations of freedom begin to erode.

As we confront these issues, Orwell's warnings in *1984* and *Animal Farm* continue to reverberate through the resistance to censorship. The proles in *1984* serve as a reminder that true power rests not in the hands of the few who seek to control thought but in the many who still possess the ability to think for themselves. Whether through lawsuits, grassroots activism, or cultural defiance, the fight for free speech is far from over. It is intensifying, as more individuals and organisations realise that the future of democracy depends not just on the right to speak, but on the courage to resist those who would silence us.

Chapter 10: Convergence with China – The West's Shift Toward Authoritarian

Speech Control

As I delve into this chapter, I am reminded of the complexities that have been building throughout this book and how the erosion of free speech, once unthinkable in democratic nations, is now unfolding before our eyes. In previous chapters, I have chronicled the slow creep of censorship, seen both in specific national contexts and across broader global trends. Yet, in this chapter, we confront one of the most unsettling developments: the convergence between Western democracies and China's authoritarian model of speech control.

China's Authoritarian Control of Free Speech

China's policies on speech suppression are not merely tools of governance but deeply institutionalised mechanisms designed to sustain the Chinese Communist Party's (CCP) power. For decades, China has operated one of the most extensive and sophisticated censorship systems in the world. The *Great Firewall*, a term as Orwellian as the concept it represents, is the state's digital battlement, designed to restrict access to foreign websites, filter online discourse, and block any content that could incite dissent or challenge the Party's narrative. Here, censorship is absolute, and the control of speech is a matter of national security.

In China, this infrastructure of control does not stop with the internet. The press is a mouthpiece of the Party, social media is carefully monitored, and surveillance technologies track citizens' behaviour to an extraordinary degree. Dissent is met not just with censorship but with punishment harassment, detention, and even forced disappearance. The justification? The preservation of *harmony*. A term that Orwell would surely recognise as doublethink, this word has been co-opted to mean the opposite of its traditional sense. Rather than fostering a society of peace and balance, harmony in China is enforced by silencing all forms of criticism. This is the same justification we explored in earlier chapters on Europe and Australia, where governments use similarly euphemistic language to justify restrictions on speech in the name of social stability.

The parallels with Orwell's *1984* are inescapable. The notion of *thoughtcrime* the act of even thinking something contrary to the Party's approved doctrine is reflected in how China punishes not just speech but the very ideas behind it. The Party's control is total, and speech that deviates from the official narrative is not only forbidden but criminalised. The world is witness to how the state enforces this dominance, using technology as both sword and shield to maintain an artificial consensus of national unity.

The West's Gradual Convergence with China

Historically, Western democracies stood in stark contrast to such authoritarian regimes. Free speech was a bedrock principle, a right to be protected even when the speech in question was offensive, controversial, or even misinformed. Yet, in recent years, a shift has been taking place in a deeply troubling convergence.

Governments in the West, particularly those with left-leaning ideologies, have begun to adopt policies that mirror China's model of speech control, albeit under a different guise. In the name of inclusivity, combating hate speech, and curbing misinformation, we are witnessing a subtle erosion of the very rights that once distinguished liberal democracies from authoritarian states. While Western countries, unlike China, do not directly impose censorship through state-controlled media, they have found an effective proxy: technology companies.

Platforms such as Facebook, Google, and X (formerly Twitter) now serve as de facto regulators of public discourse, acting in partnership with governments to control what is said, shared, and consumed online. Under pressure from state authorities and advocacy groups, these tech giants use algorithms, shadow bans, and de-platforming to moderate speech that is deemed hateful, offensive, or false. What we see is a delegation of censorship of private companies acting as agents of government, doing what the state itself cannot do without violating its laws.

In earlier chapters, we explored the rise of these platforms as modern-day thought police (Chapter 7), examining how their algorithms dictate the bounds of acceptable discourse. In the United States, Canada, and the United Kingdom, this partnership between the state and tech companies is increasingly overt. Laws aimed at curbing hate speech or misinformation blur the line between free speech and censorship, making it increasingly difficult for individuals to discern where legal protections end, and corporate censorship begins.

Surveillance and Social Control: A Shared Trajectory

As we discussed in Chapter 4 on the United Kingdom's public order laws, the West has not been immune to the expansion of surveillance technology. What began as measures designed to prevent terrorism or monitor extremist activities has gradually evolved into a broader system of monitoring and regulating speech. In this, there is an undeniable convergence with China's surveillance state. While Western democracies have yet to implement facial recognition and mass data collection on the same scale as China, they are heading in that direction. We see governments using technology to monitor online behaviours, with speech that deviates from established norms flagged as "extremist" or dangerous.

In both cases, the rationale for such surveillance is strikingly similar. China justifies its actions by claiming to preserve national security and social stability. Western governments, on the other hand, appeal to the protection of democracy, national security, or the safeguarding of vulnerable groups. The arguments differ in tone but not in substance.

Soft Authoritarianism: A New Threat to Democracy

What we are seeing, in both China and the West, is the rise of what can only be described as *soft authoritarianism*. Unlike the overt totalitarianism of China, where speech is directly controlled and dissent is criminalised, the West operates under a veneer of democracy. Yet, beneath this surface, the increasing restrictions on speech, the delegation of censorship to private entities, and the growing culture of surveillance suggest that Western democracies are inching toward a model that, while not identical to China's, is alarmingly similar.

In China, there is no pretence of free speech; the state has always maintained control. In the West, however, the erosion is subtle, and that makes it even more dangerous. As I reflected in Chapter 9 on the resistance to censorship, the challenge we now face is that many of these restrictions are cloaked in the language of progressivism and inclusivity. Orwell's concept of *newspeak* where language is deliberately narrowed to limit thought is increasingly relevant in this context. Words are redefined, and the range of acceptable speech is diminished, all in the name of protecting the public from harm.

The Way Forward: Preserving Free Speech in a Time of Convergence

The convergence between China's authoritarian methods of speech control and the West's creeping authoritarianism poses a clear and present danger to the future of free discourse. In previous chapters, particularly those focusing on Australia (Chapter 6), Europe (Chapter 5), and Canada (Chapter 3), we have seen how legal frameworks intended to curb harmful speech have often led to the suppression of dissent. If the West continues this path, it risks losing the very principles that have defined its democratic character.

The key to halting this convergence lies in a renewed commitment to free speech protections. Governments must resist the temptation to use private companies as proxies for censorship, and citizens must remain vigilant against efforts to criminalise unpopular or dissenting opinions. If we allow this slide toward soft authoritarianism to continue, we may soon find ourselves in a world where speech, once the foundation of democracy, is controlled not by the people but by a select few.

In conclusion, we face a critical juncture. The West must choose whether to preserve its commitment to free expression or to follow

China down a path where speech is no longer a right but a privilege, granted only to those who conform to the approved narrative. As we move forward, it is essential to challenge this convergence and protect the free exchange of ideas that is the lifeblood of any true democracy.

Chapter 11: What Can Be Done? – A Call to Action for Voters

As we arrive at the final chapter, the erosion of free speech is not a distant threat but a pressing reality. Each preceding chapter has methodically laid out how the very fabric of open discourse is being frayed, often in the name of progress, security, or social harmony. From the rise of authoritarian speech control in the West (Chapter 10) to the complicity of technology companies (Chapter 7), we have examined how freedom of expression, once considered sacrosanct, is increasingly stifled. The question that now stands before us is simple, yet monumental: what can be done?

This chapter is not a lament but a rallying cry. We have seen how Orwell's warnings in *1984* and *Animal Farm* are not just relics of a bygone era but prescient blueprints for the very society we risk becoming. Yet, Orwell also taught us that resistance is possible. His dystopian vision was not inevitable; it was a cautionary tale, meant to inspire vigilance and action. Therefore, the answer lies not in passive acceptance but in decisive action from citizens and voters.

Choosing Politicians Who Value Free Speech

At the heart of any democratic society is the power of the vote. This power, when used wisely, can stem the tide of censorship and authoritarian control. Unfortunately, many voters have become disconnected from the political process, disengaged by a sense of futility. But the erosion of free speech is not inevitable, and the ballot box remains one of the most potent tools we must protect.

In this regard, voters must be vigilant when selecting politicians to represent them. Too often, candidates hide behind the guise of inclusivity or safety while advancing policies that curtail free expression. Therefore, it is critical to scrutinize their voting records, public statements, and political platforms with a discerning eye. Do they advocate for laws that protect free speech, or do they support legislation that allows the state to determine which speech is acceptable and which is not? It is vital to favour those who are willing to champion free expression, even when it is inconvenient or controversial, rather than those who seek to limit it under the guise of curbing "hate speech" or "misinformation" (as discussed in Chapters 2 and 4, regarding the United States and the United Kingdom).

Equally important is holding politicians accountable once they are in office. We must demand transparency in how laws affecting speech are drafted and enforced. Silence is complicity, and citizens must make their voices heard, particularly when they see encroachments upon their rights.

Defending Free Speech on Social Media

Social media platforms have become the modern-day public square, where ideas are shared, debated, and challenged. Yet, as we discussed in Chapter 7, these digital spaces are increasingly subject to the whims of technology companies and government regulation. While these platforms claim to foster open dialogue, they have simultaneously become vehicles for censorship, de-platforming, and algorithmic manipulation.

To counter this, we must engage actively on social media. Instead of retreating in the face of online "cancel culture" or censorship, we must use these platforms to advocate for free speech. This does not mean engaging in aggressive or harmful rhetoric, but it does mean standing firm in the belief that even unpopular opinions deserve a place in the public discourse.

We must also be cautious about self-censorship. The fear of being silenced or ostracised has led many to dilute their opinions or avoid controversial topics altogether. Orwell's *1984* teaches us that the greatest threat to freedom is not always external; it often comes from within. The manipulation of language and thought in *newspeak* was effective because citizens internalised it, limiting their capacity for critical thinking. In today's world, self-censorship can be just as insidious. We must resist this trend by speaking out, respectfully yet assertively, against the growing culture of conformity.

Supporting Independent Media

One of the most effective ways to safeguard free speech is to support independent media outlets. As Chapter 9 highlighted, many mainstream news organisations have become beholden to corporate or governmental interests, often tailoring their content to fit a particular narrative. This homogenisation of information stifles dissent and limits the range of perspectives available to the public.

Independent media, though often underfunded and overlooked, plays a critical role in providing diverse viewpoints. By supporting these outlets whether through subscriptions, donations, or simply sharing their content citizens can ensure that a plurality of voices continues to be heard. Moreover, holding the media accountable for its role in suppressing free expression is essential. The free press should be a bulwark against authoritarianism, not a tool for its advancement.

Resisting the Culture of Fear

Throughout this book, we have repeatedly returned to the theme of fear of offending, fear of being ostracised, and fear of retribution. This culture of fear has been instrumental in suppressing open debate, as seen in the rise of "safe spaces" and "speech codes" in universities (Chapter 8) and the draconian speech regulations in places like Europe (Chapter 5) and Australia (Chapter 6). Yet fear is a tool of control, and the only way to combat it is through courage.

To resist this culture, we must first recognise it for what it is: a means of silencing dissent. Orwell's *1984* illustrated how fear, once internalised, becomes the most effective form of control. The Party did not need to constantly monitor every citizen because the fear of being watched was enough to enforce conformity. Similarly, today's culture of fear thrives not because of overt government action but because citizens, afraid of the consequences, silence themselves.

We must reject this fear. This does not mean engaging in reckless speech or attacking others, but it does mean standing firm in the belief that freedom of expression is a right worth defending, even when it comes at a personal cost. Courage, after all, is not the absence of fear but the ability to act despite it.

Conclusion: A Return to Free Expression

As we conclude this journey through the erosion of free speech, Orwell's dystopian warnings are more relevant today than ever before. But there is hope. The erosion of free speech is not an inevitable consequence of modern society; it is a choice a series of decisions made by individuals, institutions, and governments. And just as it is a choice to curtail speech, it is also a choice to defend it.

By recognising the warning signs, as laid out in the preceding chapters, and taking decisive action, citizens in the USA, Canada, the UK, Europe, and Australia can reclaim their right to speak freely. Whether through voting for politicians who prioritise free expression, advocating for free speech on social media, supporting independent media, or resisting the culture of fear, each of us has a role to play in securing the future of democratic debate.

The time for passive acceptance is over. As Orwell warned in *1984*, "If you want a picture of the future, imagine a boot stamping on a human face forever." But this need not be our future. The power to change course lies within us if only we are willing to act before it is too late.

Epilogue: The Echoes of Orwell in Our Modern World

As I sit to write this epilogue, I cannot help but reflect on how the world I grew up in has changed. As mentioned in the foreword, I grew up in post-war Britain and was raised in a society that held free speech as a cornerstone of our democratic values freedom hard-won and carefully preserved. Back then, there was a collective understanding of the importance of open discourse. People disagreed, often passionately, but speech was rarely stifled. Now, as I look at the world today, I see these freedoms slipping away, bit by bit, under the guise of protecting society from harm. This slow erosion of free speech, which I have laid out across the chapters of this book, feels alarmingly familiar, much like the dystopian warnings of Orwell.

Throughout this book, I have tried to sound the alarm on a disturbing trend: the convergence of Western democracies with more authoritarian regimes, like China, in their control over speech. In *Chapter 10*, I explored how China's suppression of dissent has evolved into a highly institutionalized mechanism for control. Western nations, once bastions of liberty, now seem to be adopting similar justifications for limiting speech, whether it be in the name of national security, preventing "misinformation," or protecting society from "hate." It is chilling to see how quickly the Western world has moved towards a model that resembles China's, a shift that I believe Orwell would have warned us against.

For those who argue that these restrictions are a necessary part of maintaining social harmony, I urge you to revisit *Chapter 5*, where I discuss Europe's balancing act between tolerance and free expression. The good intentions behind hate speech laws and the regulation of disinformation can often spiral into overreach, criminalizing dissenting views and stifling the open debate that is so crucial to a free society. As

I illustrated in *Chapter 4*, even in my homeland, the United Kingdom, public order laws have been used to criminalize speech that merely offends. The arrest of individuals for tweets or offhand comments signals a chilling shift one that echoes Orwell's *1984*, where thought itself becomes a crime.

The digital landscape, as covered in *Chapter 7*, has also become a battleground for free speech. We now live in a world where tech giants act as modern-day thought police, regulating what we can and cannot say. Algorithms decide which voices are amplified and which are silenced. Orwell's concept of "newspeak," in which language is manipulated to restrict thought, has taken on a new form in the way algorithms shape public discourse. The silencing of dissenting voices is not always overt de-platforming and shadow banning can be insidious, happening without the public even realizing it.

Some are indeed resisting. In *Chapter 9*, I outlined how grassroots movements, civil libertarians, and political groups are pushing back against these restrictions. Yet, the resistance is fragmented, and the forces advocating for speech control seem to grow stronger by the day. Orwell's proles, as I pointed out, represent the untapped potential for societal change, but will we act before it's too late?

In the final chapter, *What Can Be Done?* I offered a call to action. It is not enough to recognize the dangers; we must take practical steps to protect our freedoms. Whether through voting for politicians who prioritize free expression, advocating for speech on social media, or supporting independent media outlets, we must act decisively. The erosion of free speech is not an inevitable consequence of modernity, but the result of complacency and fear.

Orwell once warned us that if we allowed the erosion of freedom to continue unchecked, we might wake up one day to find ourselves in a society where free thought and free speech no longer exist. In writing this book, I hope to remind readers that we are not there yet, but we are closer than we might think. The echoes of Orwell's dystopian world are growing louder, but we still have time to change course. The fate of free speech, and indeed of democracy itself, rests in our hands.

We must listen to these echoes and act.

John Shenton

End

Don't miss out!

Visit the website below and you can sign up to receive emails whenever John Shenton publishes a new book. There's no charge and no obligation.

https://books2read.com/r/B-A-RJUO-PKCBF

BOOKS 2 READ

Connecting independent readers to independent writers.

Did you love *Echos of Orwell*? Then you should read *The Empire's Warning: What Rome's Fall Tells Us About the West Today*[1] by John Shenton!

The Empire's Warning: What Rome's Fall Tells Us About the West Today is a thought-provoking exploration of the parallels between the decline of the Roman Empire and the challenges facing modern Western civilisation. Drawing on extensive historical research and personal experiences—such as walking Hadrian's Wall and visiting Roman Vindolanda—the book examines whether the West, like Rome, is destined to fall or if it can learn from history and avert a similar fate.

The book begins by comparing the Roman Empire at its zenith to the post-World War II West, which, like Rome, has enjoyed unparalleled dominance in military, economic, and cultural influence. Yet, just as

1. https://books2read.com/u/mdaQZ5

2. https://books2read.com/u/mdaQZ5

Rome's decline came in slow, subtle stages, so too do the signs of Western decay. Political instability, economic stagnation, military overreach, and the breakdown of public trust are examined in detail, offering readers a compelling account of the present-day West through the lens of history.

Chapters such as The Role of Governance and Economic Stagnation and the Collapse of Infrastructure delve into the systemic issues that contributed to Rome's downfall, highlighting alarming similarities in Western governance, corruption, and fiscal irresponsibility. Immigration and Integration offers an in-depth analysis of how mass migration destabilised the Roman Empire and draws comparisons to contemporary immigration challenges in the West.

As the book progresses, it asks whether the West can reverse its current trajectory. In Can Decline Be Reversed?, historical lessons from figures like Diocletian and Constantine are explored, along with modern policy recommendations for economic reform, political renewal, and societal cohesion. The final chapter, The Future of Western Civilisation: Decline or Transformation?, poses the question of whether Western society can transform itself in the face of technological disruption, geopolitical shifts, and cultural decay.

Ultimately, The Empire's Warning is a call to action. While the story of Rome is a cautionary tale, the book remains cautiously optimistic, offering insights on how the West might rejuvenate itself through bold reforms and renewed civic duty. In a world of growing uncertainty, this book challenges readers to reflect on the future of their civilisation and the lessons history has to offer.

Also by John Shenton

Business Plan Basics
The Bahamas - More Islands and Recipes Than You Expect!
Collected Musings from Bricks and Mortar to E-commerce
The Smart City Odyssey: Unveiling the Secrets to Traveller-Centric
Software
The Dragon's Gambit: China's Bid for Global Dominance and the
Western Response
Silent Weapon
Business Basics: Money Sources
Influx
Fried Chips
Mandates, Motors, and Misinformation
Echos of Orwell
Control and Chaos
The Empire's Warning: What Rome's Fall Tells Us About the West
Today

About the Author

John Shenton was born in Birmingham, England and grew up in postwar England. He spent several years as a Radio Officer onboard a variety of vessels sailing to the Persian Gulf, the Indian Ocean and South China seas.

With degrees and a background in electronics and computers he has lived and worked within the United Kingdom, Germany, Switzerland and Canada.

While doing so, he established numerous trading relationships in Japan, Korea, the USA, China and other countries.

He has been retired for some time now living in Montréal Canada enjoying golfing, writing, sailing and many other things automotive.

About the Publisher

John Shenton published via Draft2digital